W9-AQP-509

DAVY CROCKETT'S
EARTHQUAKE

WILLIAM O. STEELE

DAVY CROCKETT'S EARTH QUAKE

Illustrated by Nicolas

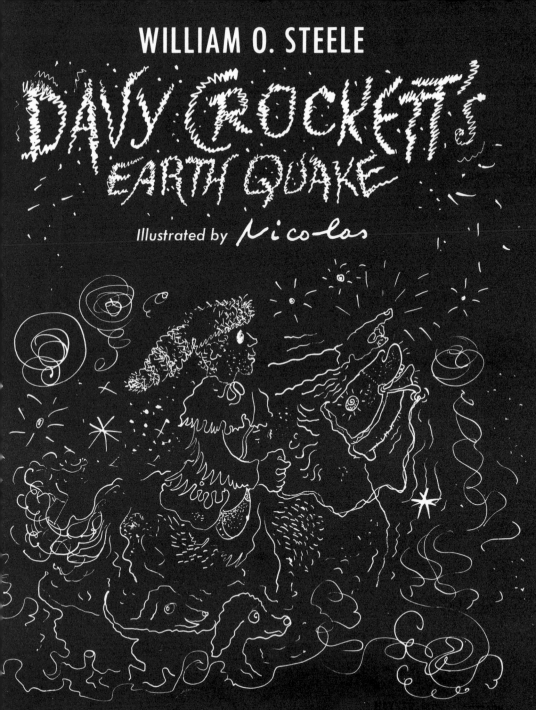

HARCOURT, BRACE & WORLD, INC., NEW YORK

AUTHOR'S NOTE

This is a story that might have been. In the fall of 1811 nobody seems to know exactly where Davy was, or what he was doing. He might have been bear hunting in West Tennessee when the New Madrid earthquake was changing up the landscape, and the Great Comet of 1811 was lighting up the sky. So all of this story might have been true, except that bit about Rattler whistling *The British Soldier*. That was just a plumb lie. Rattler never learned to whistle.

E.2.66

LIBRARY OF CONGRESS CATALOG CARD NUMBER: 56-6920

PRINTED IN THE UNITED STATES OF AMERICA BY
THE MURRAY PRINTING COMPANY, FORGE VILLAGE, MASSACHUSETTS

For Allerton William Steele, who shot 206 tall tales in one year and lived to tell it.

One

Sunrise made red and yellow streaks up the sky. The hound, Whirlwind, stood up and stretched. He yawned and all the other hounds yawned too. The door of the log cabin swung open and a tall man came out. His eyes were blue and he wore a coonskin cap. His name was Davy Crockett.

"Now, Whirlwind," he said. "I'll just put a little piece of that sunrise in my pocket for luck. For today me and you are going hunting in West Tennessee. And I aim to kill two thousand bears afore I come home."

Davy turned around and looked into the cabin. His wife knelt on the hearth baking ash cake for his journey. And his two little boys sat side by side in bed with their yellow hair sticking up all whichaways.

"Pappy," called the oldest boy. "Do you have to go way off to West Tennessee and hunt bears? Couldn't you stay here and play with me and William? We can wrastle as good as any bear."

Davy stepped back into the cabin. "Oh, you're mighty fine wrastlers, you are, for a fact," he remarked. "But don't you know there ain't nary bear left around here in Franklin County? And don't you know there's so many bears in West Tennessee the poor critters don't have room to grow? There's such a crowd of them that half of them bears have to hold their breath so the other half can have enough room to breathe."

The little boys' eyes grew round. "Pappy, is that a fact?" asked William.

"Why, boys," Davy went on, "I can hear those bears at night, a-moaning and groaning because they are so crowded and squeezed up together. And every now and then one will lift up his head and holler, 'Davy come a-running and shoot some of these fat fellers before we all get squoze to death!' So you see, I just got to get to West Tennessee."

"Let me go with you!" cried the youngest boy. "I ain't never shot a bear."

"Nor me, neither," spoke up John. "And I'm nigh four years old."

Davy laughed and grabbed up his two little boys, one under each arm. He spun around and around, faster than a spinning wheel. The boys yelled with joy. Then one climbed down and sat on Davy's feet, and the other scrambled up to his shoulders. Davy hopped across the room like a frog, giving a big war whoop at every hop.

"Now, stop," cried Mrs. Polly Crockett. "You'll shake the shingles off the roof and the soot out of the chimney. You'll spoil the ash cake and scare the crickets."

Davy stood his young 'uns on their heads in the middle of the bed.

"Boys," he said, "I can't take you with me this time. You got to stay home. Who would look after Mammy, if you didn't stay? Who would fetch the wood and water for her? And who on earth would keep the varmints away from the cabin?"

"Pappy!" shouted John. "Do you think a painter will try to get in the cabin?"

"No," answered Davy. "There won't be no painters around. But there might be a rumsquaddle creeping about. I saw a rumsquaddle's tracks down near the spring last week."

"What's a rumsquaddle?" asked William in a whisper.

"Why, a rumsquaddle is a fee-rocious varmint," answered Davy. "He's round and striped at both ends and tall and hairy in the middle and sort of different everywhere else."

"What will we do if the rumsquaddle comes?" asked the youngest boy. "We ain't got a rifle."

"We could wrastle him," suggested John.

Davy shook his head. "He's too greasy to wrastle. You couldn't get a good hold on him," he told them. "And you can't shoot a rumsquaddle neither. The hide's too tough. Even a silver bullet won't go through it. But listen close now, for this is the way to kill a rumsquaddle. When you hear one sniffing around outside the cabin, you set out a barrel of popcorn and a barrel of water. The rumsquaddle will eat the popcorn and drink the water. The popcorn will swell up inside of him and he'll get bigger . . . and bigger! Finally he'll blow up into a ske-dillion pieces!"

"Whooo---eeee!" yelled the boys. "We sure hope a rum-squaddle comes around."

"And now this here ash cake is ready," said Mrs. Polly. "The sun's up, Davy, and it's time to go."

Davy grabbed up his two boys in a big squeeze. They pulled him down on to the bed. The three of them rolled and tumbled about till the shucks rattled out of the mattress to the floor.

"That wrastle will have to do you till I come home at Christmas time," Davy told them.

He picked up his saddlebags and all the Crocketts went

outdoors. Davy's horse was ready and waiting. His bear dogs, Whirlwind and Rattler, were waiting to go hunting with him. The sun was swinging at a right smart gait up through the hills.

Davy flung the saddlebags on his horse's back behind the pack of supplies. He kissed his wife and two boys.

"Call up the rest of the hounds, boys," he said, "and take them inside the cabin. Keep the door closed tight so they can't follow me. Be good and I'll bring you each a jim-dandy necklace of bear claws."

"Goodbye, Pappy," cried William. "Kill a heap of bears."

"Goodbye, Pappy," John called. "Be back by Christmas time so I can shoot your rifle, Old Betsy, and celebrate Christmas morning."

"Nothing in creation can keep me away," Davy told them.

The boys whistled the other hounds into the cabin and shut the door.

"Goodbye, Polly," Davy said to his wife. "I hate to leave you. But I'll bring home a heap of meat and skins. There's plenty of bacon hanging on the rafters and corn enough in the barn to keep you till I return. And I'll be back by Christmas."

"Goodbye, Davy," she answered. "Don't worry about us. We'll be safe as bumblebees. But oh, we'll miss you something fierce, so hurry home."

"I will," promised Davy. He gave a tug on the lead line and the horse followed him down the trail. Whirlwind and Rattler trotted alongside.

"Well, we're off," Davy said to Whirlwind.

And just to keep himself company he began to sing a little tune:

> *"Hey diddle-dum-do-dinkety-do,*
> *The bears are on the vine,*
> *As thick and ripe as pumpkin fleas*
> *And sweet as sour wine."*

At the top of the next hill he looked back. His cabin lay in shadows, for the sun was not yet up high enough to shine on it. A whip-poor-will called down in the corn field. And dew lay thick on the red maples and yellow hickory trees.

"Now, fare-ye-well, old whip-poor-will," called Davy. "And fare-ye-well, my wife and my fine boys and my snug little cabin. For I'm off to Chickasaw Injun country to hunt bears, and good luck must go with me."

Two

Davy traveled fast. As he went along the trail, turkeys fed
on acorns and deer browsed beneath the big gold beech trees.
Davy gave them all "Howdy," except one fat gobbler that
he shot for his dinner.

And that night while he slept, a comet swung through
the heavens. It was big and bright and lit up all one corner
of the sky. The horse saw it and whinnied in alarm, but
Davy and the hounds slept peacefully on.

The next day Davy said to the hounds Whirlwind and
Rattler, "Tonight we'll come to the Tennessee River. And
there'll be a tavern on the river bank, I reckon. We'll sleep
there, if there's a bed to be had."

But that afternoon Davy met a man on the trace. The man was holding his head and groaning at every step.

"Can I help you any way, stranger?" asked Davy, moving aside.

But the man groaned and went on without answering. And by and by Davy met a second man, and this one was hobbling along with a stick and wailing with pain.

"Is there anything I can do for you, friend?" Davy wanted to know. But the man shook his head and limped away.

And presently here came a third man with a bloody bandage round his head and his broken arm dangling. Once more Davy made room for the man to pass.

But as the traveler went by, Davy spoke a third time. "Friend," he asked, "has there been an Injun raid back that way? Was it a hurricane or a plague of hoopsnakes?"

"Ohhhh," groaned the man. "It was worse than all three of those put together. Turn back, friend, while you are still well and whole."

And the man went on down the trail.

"Well, now," said Davy, "it must be something terrible up ahead. It may be I'll get in trouble if I go on. But if my two fists let me down, why, I've a very fine rifle. And if my rifle misfires, I've still got two fighting dogs. And if my dogs turn tail, my pockets are oozing with good luck, and *that* ain't failed me yet. I'll just see what this trouble is."

So Davy went on. And pretty soon he came to the banks

of the wide Tennessee and there stood a tavern. A sign over the door read THE ACHING TOOTH. "Now that's a fine name for an inn," said Davy.

Just at that moment the door to the tavern flew open and one, two, three men came flying out and landed in the weeds at Davy's feet.

One picked himself up and limped off, one lay on the ground moaning and groaning, but the third one didn't do anything for he was knocked out cold as a cucumber.

"Mister," said Davy to the second man. "What's going on here?"

The man groaned and sat up. "The Eye-Gouger . . ." he moaned, ". . . has a most . . . terrible . . . strummifying . . . toothache."

"Who's the Eye-Gouger?" asked Davy.

"Why, he runs the tavern," answered the man, and with another groan he rolled over into the blackberry bushes.

"Well, he's got a mighty peculiar way of entertaining his customers," said Davy. "He's got no call to clutter up the river bank this way. I'll just go tell him so."

He walked up to the tavern door and went in. The room was dark and the tavern keeper stood behind a table. He was a big man with long black hair and a red and swollen face.

"What do you want?" he growled at Davy. "Whatever 'tis, you won't get it here. I got a most terrible strummifying toothache, and fighting is the only thing that helps it.

17

So fighting is the only thing you'll get here this day."

"Now that's too bad," said Davy. "I came to cure your toothache, but if fighting's all you've got to offer, I'll be on my way."

"Oh, oh, oh!" screamed the Eye-Gouger, holding his jaw. "Oh, how it hurts! Don't go away, stranger. If you can cure my toothache, you can have a week's lodging free and the seat closest to the fire in the evenings.

"But if you don't cure my toothache, you must stand up and fight like a man," he said, and he smiled a horrible smile and held up his right thumbnail. It was four inches long and honed sharp as a razor. "I'm called the Eye-Gouger and this is my weapon. I'm rough as flint rocks and meaner than a poke of rattlesnakes."

He threw a feather up in the air and sliced it in half with his sharpened thumbnail.

Davy didn't like the look of that thumbnail. It could flip a man's eyeball out of its socket quicker than a wink. But he only smiled and shook hands on the bargain, for he could feel good luck curled on his shoulder like a cat.

Davy and the Eye-Gouger went out in the stable yard. Davy brought a team of six strong mules out of the stable and hitched them together.

"Now," he said to the inn keeper. "You take hold of that stump there and I'll tie the mule traces to the tooth. Then when I give the word, the mules will pull and the tooth will come flying out."

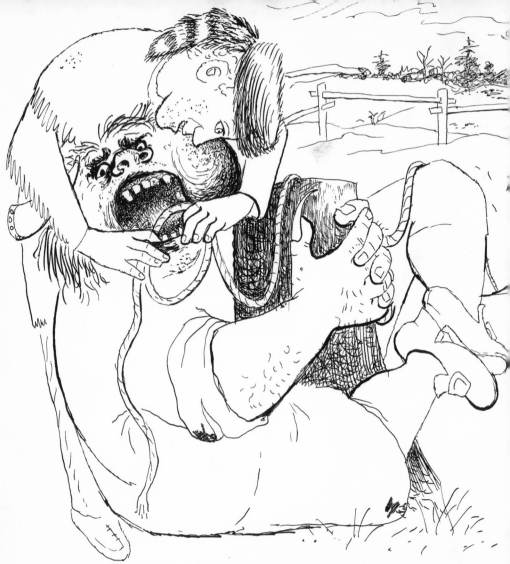

So the Eye-Gouger sat down and wrapped his arms and
legs around the stump. He opened his mouth wide. Davy
could see his teeth as big as millstones sitting in his ugly
red gums. The teeth were crowded right close together and

try as he might Davy couldn't get those traces tied around the bad tooth. He tried every kind of a knot and noose, but it wouldn't work.

"Uwwy up!" said the Eye-Gouger.

"Well," said Davy, "if one way won't work, another will."

He whipped out his hatchet and fetched the tooth a good clip.

The Eye-Gouger howled and unwound himself from the stump. "Now I'm a-going to kill you," he told Davy. "I'm going to have your bones for breakfast and make soap out of the rest of you!"

The Eye-Gouger roared and came slashing at Davy with his sharp eye-gouging fingernail. That fingernail made

Davy real thoughtful, so he bit it off, clean down to the quick.

Then the Eye-Gouger was really mad. He grabbed Davy by his nose and flung him twice around his head and threw him down hard. Davy lay on the ground and the trees were spinning around him like a whirligig.

"Now I can't hardly let this inn keeper jump up and down on me," thought Davy. "For it might make me tired and then I'd be a long time getting after them bears and them bears would be so disappointed."

So he grabbed hold of a hickory tree that was whirling by and that stopped the spinning. And he raised up his feet and gave the Eye-Gouger a most tremendous kick right under his third shirt button. The wind whooshed out of the Eye-Gouger and caused a small hurricane down along the Tombigbee River in Alabama.

Davy jumped to his feet and the Eye-Gouger ran at him with his head lowered like a buffalo's and butted Davy so hard he near about knocked Davy's gizzard crooked.

And then the Eye-Gouger up and kicked Davy tarnal hard in the shins twice and almost made Davy mad. So Crockett grabbed the Eye-Gouger by his long hair and twirled him around and around and threw him head first against the cowshed.

And Davy strolled over and jerked the Eye-Gouger up off the ground. "Now this here is old Doctor Crockett's Electrifying Cure for Strummifying Toothaches," he said.

And drawing back his fist Davy let the Eye-Gouger have it smack-o in the jaw and teeth sailed out of his mouth every whichaways.

After a minute or so the Eye-Gouger stood up and grinned at Davy.

"Stranger," he hollered. "I can give you a bag of gold or a fine black horse or a suit of clothes made from catfish skins. I'll give you anything you name, for you've knocked out each and every one of my teeth and I'll never have a toothache again."

And he grabbed Davy up in such a bear hug that the coonskin cap on Davy's head let out a yip.

"No, thankee kindly," Davy answered. "All I'm after is a meal and a night's lodging, for tomorrow I aim to cross the river and go bear hunting."

"Then come in and welcome," said the Eye-Gouger. "My floors are as soft as a feather bed and I've got mashed turnips that taste like the best kind of deer-meat pie."

So Davy slept in the inn called *The Aching Tooth*, and overhead the comet burned across the skies.

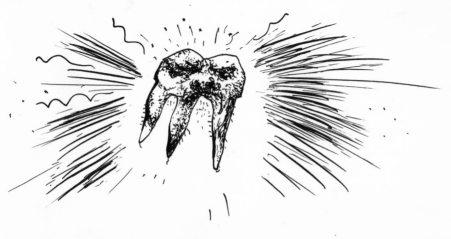

Three

The first day Davy traveled into Chickasaw country he saw a heap of bears. Bears were rolling on the ground, sleeping in the trees and playing blindman's buff along the creek banks. Davy could hardly walk for bumping into more bears. But he made his way through them as best he could, for these bears were poorly with no meat on their ribs.

The second day Crockett found bears eating acorns and beechnuts, digging worms to go fishing and scratching their fat sides on every tree.

So he made camp right there in the middle of these fine, fat, frisky bears. Every day he went hunting. And the thick, soft hides by his campfire made a tall pile.

"Oh, I'm the luckiest man alive right this minute," Davy told Whirlwind. "For I can take back a heap of meat to my boys and sell many a bear skin at the store for pretties for Polly."

One day Davy and his dogs were out hunting and they came to a canebrake. A big fat bear came waddling out. Davy raised his gun to shoot. But as soon as the bear saw Old Betsy it knew the end had come and skedaddled into the woods.

"Now, I won't bother to chase that bear," commented Davy. "I'll not stretch my legs for a bear that ain't willing to stand up and be shot proper."

That bear was so scared it began to run in a big five mile circle around Davy. It passed him twice in an hour. Davy went on about his hunting.

But a week later Crockett and the dogs happened by the same place. And there was that fat bear running in the same circle. It had gone around so many times that it had worn a trench seven feet deep.

Davy could see the poor critter had lost all its fat and was no more than skin and bones.

"I'll shoot that bear and put it out of its misery," remarked Davy. "For it's so scared it'll never stop running."

So he shot it next time around. And sure enough when he jumped down into the trench to bring up the bear, it was so poorly he could lift it with one hand. And the truth was it had starved to death three days beforehand.

The next day Davy spied ten bears playing leapfrog in

a ring. "I'll just join the fun," Davy told Rattler and Whirlwind. "And you two scout around for more bears."

So Davy slipped into the ring and the bears paid him no heed, for the fact was Davy looked a little bit like a bear.

The game went on and Davy bent over with his hands on his knees and the bears went sailing over, one after another. When Davy's turn came, he slipped his tomahawk from his belt. As he jumped over each bear, he gave it a wham on the head. When he'd gone around the circle, there lay ten dead bears.

"I expect they was tired of playing leapfrog anyhow," Davy said.

So the days went by. In the evenings Crockett sat near the campfire smoking the bear meat and pegging out fresh skins to dry in the heat. And sometimes he gave lessons in bear hunting to Rattler. For Whirlwind was an old dog and knew more about bear hunting than Davy himself. But Rattler was young and bumptious and sometimes figured he knew more than he really did.

"Now this is what you do when you find two bears sleeping close together," Davy told Rattler. "You come up real quiet and tie their tails together. Make a good firm knot, Rattler. Then you haul off with a loud war whoop. The bears jump up and start to run off in opposite directions. But they find something holding to their tails. And they get scared something awful. They strain and pull and jerk so hard to get away that their skins come right off. And then you've got two bear skins without firing a shot or using a skinning knife. Ain't that right, Whirlwind?"

Whirlwind nodded but Rattler just chewed a bone. He had his own notions about tying bears' tails together.

And in the sky, every night, the comet shone brighter.

But by and by a day came when Crockett couldn't find any more bears. He and Whirlwind hunted north and he and Rattler hunted south. But nary a bear came grunting through the woods. Nary a bear left its paw marks in the mud of the creek banks.

"Them bears have left the country," remarked Davy with a chuckle. "When they found out it was me and Old

Betsy after them, they high tailed it out of here. But there's nary a place a bear can go that I can't follow."

So he packed up his truck and set out westward, singing:

"Oh the Chickasaw bear has gone for good,
Hitched up his wagon and drove through the wood,
Packed up his fiddle and his fish bone bow—
And can't be found neither high nor low.
Hey diddle-dum-do-dinkety-do."

In two days Crockett came to a place where bear tracks were all over the place and bear scratches on every tree. "Now here I'll make camp," he told the dogs. "A few more skins and I'll set out for home."

For in truth Davy missed his pretty wife and two boys. A campfire in the bare woods of winter is a lonesome thing. Many an evening Davy thought about the well-chinked walls of his cabin and the hot ash cake baking on the hearth. And many a day he thought about his little yellow headed young 'uns fighting rumsquaddles at home.

Now it wasn't often that Davy Crockett got fooled. But this time he'd been fooled for certain. Though there were bear signs everywhere, there weren't any bears. He looked around right sharp and never saw a bear. It made him uneasy.

Then it was something stood up on his shoulder, yawned and stretched. It jumped down and bounded off into the woods, looking mighty like his good luck. And that made him uneasier yet.

"Things is mighty queersome here," he muttered.

It was late in the day. Davy went straightaway to camp. He didn't give Rattler any lessons, because he'd been fooled mighty bad. He built no fire. He and Whirlwind and Rattler ate a cold supper. They lay down together to sleep and Davy pulled some bearskins over them, for it was a cold night.

An old owl asked Davy, "Whoooo cooks for you?"

"Sometimes I do," Crockett answered. "But mostly my pretty wife Polly cooks for me. Now go to sleep."

And the woods were quiet so Davy and the dogs went to sleep.

In the middle of the night the dogs began to stir. The horse began to stamp its feet. And the dogs lifted up their noses and howled.

Davy woke up and jumped out of the furs. "The woods is afire!" he cried, for it was light as day.

But it wasn't a fire. It was the comet, swinging down low through the treetops and shaking its long fiery tail. Davy felt a cold shiver of fear go up and down his spine like a snake, for he'd not seen a comet before.

Davy watched for a long time. "I'd shoot that comet with Old Betsy," he muttered, "but it's liable to bust to pieces and fall down here. It might set the woods afire, for a fact. I'd best leave it where it is."

So he covered up again and went back to sleep.

In the morning Davy could still see the comet burning

with a greenish light in the sky. "Go to hang!" said Davy to the comet, shaking his fist at it.

But the comet only burned a little brighter.

Davy went to look at his heap of skins. And now he was fit to be tied. For the creek had come up in the night and soaked all the bearskins.

"Boys," he said to the dogs, "things ain't going right around here. A creek ain't supposed to overflow in dry weather. But this one did and ruined my skins. I'll give them bears one more chance to show up. And if'n I don't shoot a bear this day, I'll leave for home tomorrow."

He turned around and gave a big grin. "Boys," he said. "Let's not be hasty. For yonder comes the biggest bear in all Tennessee to bid us good-morning."

The bear didn't hang back and act bashful. It came on at a good clip and showed Davy what fine pretty teeth it had.

Davy took a look at that bear down the length of his rifle barrel. He aimed careful, right smack at the bear's heart and pulled the trigger. Old Betsy hollered but the ball took a sidewise leap and went around that bear!

"And now I'm going to leave!" cried Crockett, and he turned to go.

But the bear grabbed him by his shirttail and swung him around. Davy reached for his knife, but the bear wasn't eager to let him use it. He put his fat forelegs around Davy and hugged him tight. Davy's ribs got to know each other real well.

Davy and the bear fell on the ground and rolled over and over. Several trees had to step aside so they wouldn't be knocked down. Every time Davy got on top he bit a hunk out of that bear. And every time the bear got on top he scratched Davy backward and forward and twice across the face.

Finally Crockett got an arm loose and stabbed that bear three times with his knife. But the bear just laughed. He leaned way over with his tongue hanging out and laughed real hearty. So Davy got both hands loose and grabbed that bear's tongue and wrapped it four times around the varmint's neck and choked that bear plumb to death before he could so much as let out a growl.

Davy lay on the ground for a spell. It may be he admired the scenery. And when he got up he took the barrel off his rifle and went to the creek and laid the barrel in the running water.

"For Old Betsy's been witched," he told Rattler. "She never missed like that before. And running water will unwitch a gun, wash the witch spell clean away."

He stooped over to pick up the rifle barrel. But something slipped from his pocket and fell into the creek. He could see it lying there, gleaming and glistening, looking mighty like his good luck piece of sunrise. But try as he might he couldn't fetch it up.

And overhead the comet burned brighter and brighter in the winter sky.

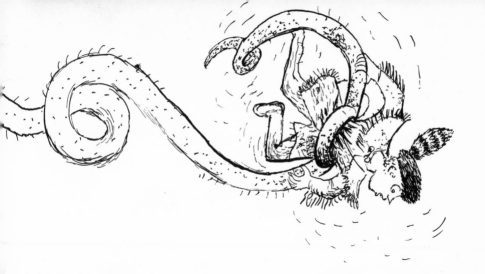

Four

Davy wasted no time. He loaded his skins, wet as they were, whistled up his dogs and set out for home.

"My luck's gone," Davy thought. "Not curled up on my shoulder or warming up my pocket. My rifle's witched and things has taken an uncommon queer turn. The bears have all gone off to get their teeth and claws sharpened and I don't aim to wait around till they get back."

He glanced up at the comet shining green and yellow in the sky. "Go back where you belong," Davy bellowed. "I'm going home. How about you going too?"

But the comet sailed on across the blue sky, bright as a flash of gunpowder. "I know in reason that critter is the cause of all these goings-on," Davy grumbled.

That night Crockett camped beside a spring that bubbled from under a flat rock. He built up a big fire to hide the shine of the comet. And he made a good hot stew and gave the dogs each a big share.

Then he lay down to sleep, and while he slept he dreamed. He dreamed that he had hired himself out to a monstrous big old bear. The bear was mean-looking as an overseer and his eyes were little and ugly. He put Davy to work with some other folks planting pumpkins.

The ground was powerful rich and every time Davy poked a seed into the ground he had to jump back to keep from getting knocked down by the fast growing vine.

He worked and worked, and he was beginning to get tired. But every time he tried to take a rest that bear would look at him and snarl. So Davy kept right on working.

But by and by an awful thing happened. He pushed one of the pumpkin seeds into the ground and it had hardly touched the dirt before it began to grow. You never saw such a fine plant, as thick as a man's arm, and growing every second.

Davy stepped back out of the way but the vine came after him. It reached out for him every way he turned and then it caught him by the feet.

Crockett let out a whoop and fought mightily to get away. The vine just grabbed him tighter and tighter. He drew out his hunting knife and tried to cut the vine, slashing at it with all his might. But the vine wrapped around his arm and squeezed till the knife dropped from his hand. Now it had him by the waist. It lifted him up in the air and shook him and shook him. . . .

Davy woke up. He felt around his waist. No pumpkin vine had hold of him. But something was shaking the living daylights out of him and making a terrible racket into the bargain—crashing and groaning and shrieking.

Davy put up his hands to cover his ears, but his head was rattling around so he could not lay hold of it. Rattler and Whirlwind were trying hard to climb inside his shirtfront.

And the worst thing of all was the way the earth kept shaking and shivering and humping up and turning over. Davy's head went round till he felt like a Junebug on a string.

"It's an earthquake!" cried Crockett. The dogs didn't believe him, for it was easy seen that nothing as terrible as this would have a common name like that.

The ground rose and fell under them like a creek riffling over a stretch of shoals. Davy grabbed Whirlwind by the ear and Whirlwind grabbed Rattler by the leg and Rattler grabbed Davy by his shirttail and they all held on tight.

Trees crashed all around them and the wind went whistling by with a sound like a hag-ridden ghost. The horse gave a scream and went tearing off into the bushes.

"Now he can run if he's a mind to," said Davy. "And I might run too if my legs would listen to me. But running won't help, for this is the end of the world, I'm certain sure." The hounds looked glad to hear it would soon be over.

The earth jumped up in the air and kicked its heels a little. "Oh, I wish I was home with my wife and boys," cried Davy. "For the end of the world don't come often and I would like to be there to talk to them about it."

Some more trees crashed down and a heap of deer came running by, bleating most pitifully. Bears scampered round and round with their eyes shooting sparks, catamounts screamed, and all kinds of little varmints streaked by.

The sky was a queer yellow color and the comet spread its tail from one end of the sky to the other. Oh, it was a fearsome sight.

Davy got up on his hands and knees and the hounds crouched on each side of him. The wind howled and the wild animals cried and the earth shook and shook.

"Now Rattler and Whirlwind are most scared out of their wits," Davy told himself. "I'll have to tell them something to keep their minds off their troubles. I'll tell 'em how to plant potatoes, for it's a useful thing to know."

"Boys," he shouted. "You plant 'taters in the dark of the moon. First you cut up the seed 'tater. . . ."

A rock went whistling over their heads.

"And you make sure each piece has an eye in it, else it won't make no 'taters."

A tree crashed right beside them.

"You dig a fair sized hole," Davy went on, but the earth began to shiver and shake worse than ever. And right where Davy and the hounds were huddled together, the ground

split wide open like a watermelon dropped from a considerable height.

Davy made a leap and scrambled out of the crack and the hounds came right behind him. "Boys," said Davy. "I never cared much for 'taters nohow!"

The earthquake went on for a good spell. But finally it slackened up and the shaking wasn't so bad. What trees were left standing looked as though they might go on standing a while longer. Near Davy a bear and two deer still crouched together in terror, and a rattlesnake was comforting two rabbits and a catamount. A mother turkey had settled her wings over a family of little possums.

Then the wind died down and the varmints went whimpering off into the bushes instead of sitting with their arms around each other.

Now the shaking had almost stopped. The earth just twitched every now and then like an old dog chasing rabbits in its sleep.

Davy and Rattler and Whirlwind stood up. Davy looked all about. Things had changed up right smart. Trees were tumbled every whichaway; the ground was humped up here and split open there; creeks were flowing backward and some had left their beds entirely, leaving fish gaping on the mud and crawdads easing around looking miserable.

"Well, now, that was a heap of commotion," remarked Davy. "I reckon I've lost my horse and my skins and all my gear. I've lost my good bear hams and smoked sidemeat. But I'm still alive. I've still got my rifle-gun and my two dogs. And if I get home and find my wife and boys safe and sound, why, I'll count myself the luckiest man in creation."

Five

Davy set out once more. It was a long way to go with no pot in which to cook his supper and no blankets to cover him at night. But a man has never yet brought back what was lost by sitting in the woods and crying. So he walked on.

It was a queersome day. First it was hot and then it was cold. The wind blew something wonderful and then the air would be so still even cattail fluff wouldn't float. The sky was striped green and white like a grass snake. The ground shook and growled and hiccupped.

Crockett tried to hurry for he was anxious to see his family. But the ground was rough and torn up and trees lay everywhere, barring the way. He had to dodge and twist and turn and hop over and go around and duck under until several times Davy met himself coming back the other way.

Once he came to a place where the earth was as wrinkled as the skin of a dried apple. Great cracks ran this way and that. Some of the cracks were much too wide to jump. Davy had to walk many miles around them.

Then he came to the biggest crack of all. It widened and widened and in the widest part was a little island. And on the island were two huckleberry bushes and a baby deer. The fawn bleated at Davy most pitifully.

"Now that's a shame," said Davy to Whirlwind. "For that fawn can't get across the crack. And it's bound to starve to death unless it falls in the crack. One way or the other, it's a dead deer."

Davy walked on, shaking his head. He had to hurry on home. There was still a far journey before him. But the deer let out a high quivering call. Davy stopped. He knew he was done for. He had to go back and rescue that deer.

He turned back to look at the gaping earth. "Now how in the name of General Jackson can I get across that great split?" he asked himself aloud.

Rattler sat down and scratched his ribs. Whirlwind put his head on one side and pondered. If there was one thing Whirlwind liked to do, it was to think out the answers to hard problems.

Davy didn't reckon he could possibly jump across. He

couldn't swim for there was no water. He couldn't fly, for he'd never learned how.

There was a great, huge, old pine tree nearby. Quick as a wink Crockett took out his hatchet and began to chop at the tree. It was such a big tree he worked most of that day before he was able to chop through the trunk. But along about suppertime the pine started to fall.

Crockett and the hounds went on to bed. The next morning that tree was still falling. And that pine was so tall it didn't hit the island till afternoon. It fell spang between the huckleberry bushes. Davy was mighty pleased with his aim for that was where he wanted the tree to land.

So Davy ran out to the island and whisked up the little deer. He came teetering back across the pine log and put the fawn down. It scampered off with its tail standing up as brave as a fife and drum corps and Davy laughed to see it go. Then he started for home once more.

By and by he heard a noise off in some bushes. It was a little whimpering sound. Whirlwind went to see what it was, but Rattler stayed with Davy. Rattler knew about all kinds of queer things that sat in the bushes and whimpered and this wasn't the day he cared to meet them.

But Whirlwind kept on nosing about. "Come away, Whirlwind, we got to hurry on," called Davy. "I reckon it's a bear cub that's looking for its mammy."

Whirlwind looked thoughtful. It might be a bear cub, but it didn't smell quite right. So Crockett came to look too.

And there in the bushes sat a little blackhaired, black-eyed young 'un.

"A little Injun cub!" cried Davy. "And most nigh scared to death. Where do you reckon he came from?"

The Indian boy didn't say anything. One big tear rolled down his cheek.

Davy smiled. This little boy was the same age as his own youngest. He ought to be able to cheer him up. So he waggled his ears and stood on his head, but the little boy stared back as solemn as a preacher.

Davy watched him. "Well, now, you don't look much like my little tow-headed young 'uns," he said at last. "But I reckon your pappy and mammy think just as much of you as I think of my boys. So I'll just have to make sure your pappy gets you back, same as I'd want him to bring home my boys, did he find 'em in an earthquake."

So he swung the little boy up to his shoulder. And he

turned away from the path that led toward home and took the trail south to find the Chickasaw Indians.

Crockett's long steps covered the miles and every step he took carried him farther from home. And he was mighty worried for nary an Indian did he see, nor signs of any.

By and by he came to a riverbed. The water had all run off and left a heap of mud in its place. Davy scratched his head. "I'll have to wade right across here," he said. "I don't mind getting my toes muddy."

He settled the Indian boy firmly on his shoulder and started over. The mud came to his knees. Davy waded on. Soon the mud reached his waist, then it climbed as high as his chest.

Davy stood the boy up on his shoulders and went on. The mud got steadily deeper—up to Davy's chin, then to his eyes, and soon it was over his head. The going was hard but he pushed on through.

Finally the mud got so deep Davy had to hold Old Betsy up and let the little Indian stand on the very end of the rifle. And even so, only his head stuck up out of the riverbed.

Davy just walked along with his steady gait. The mud got thicker and thicker till finally it was so thick Davy couldn't push through it.

"This won't do," said Davy, and he whipped out his ax and began to chop his way through the mud. Now Davy was a powerful chopper, and it wasn't long till he'd chopped his way clean on across the riverbed and out on the other side.

When he stood on the bank at last, he reached up and held Old Betsy steady while the little Indian boy jumped down. There they stood on the riverbank, Davy and the Indian boy and Old Betsy and the hounds, all covered up with mud from head to toe. Even the little boy had his ears full of mud.

And the mud was so thick and so tough, they couldn't get it off no matter how they rubbed and scraped. Finally Davy had to take his hunting knife and skin every one of them out of those mud pelts, just like he'd skin a deer!

Toward evening they came to a spring. An Indian woman knelt by the spring filling a pot with water.

The little boy leaped grasshopper-like from Crockett's shoulder and ran to his mammy. His mammy grabbed up her little boy and hugged him tight. And Davy turned and went quietly on his way.

"I'll not wait for thanks," he told the hounds. "For I don't want any. And I got to make tracks and get for home."

On through the bright night he went. And in four days time he came to the banks of the wide Tennessee.

He did not stop at the inn called *The Aching Tooth* for fear that the Eye-Gouger might have grown a new set of aching teeth. Davy didn't care to waste time doctoring.

Not far from the inn he came to a most tremendous sycamore log. Now Davy in his day had seen many a hollow sycamore of right good size, but this one had them all beat.

Its hollow branches covered several acres of ground, going this way and that.

Crockett stared at the log. And presently he could see something moving down in the dark spaces of that tree. Pretty soon the thing came closer and Davy could make out it was a man. The man walked out of the log and sat down on the ground. He looked tired and sad.

"Stranger, can I be of any service to you?" asked Davy politely. "For it's easy seen some kind of trouble sits heavy on your shoulders."

"Aye," the man nodded. "I've got a heap of trouble. But I doubt if you could help. My old one-horned cow has wandered into this log and got plumb lost. And I've searched and searched, but I can't find hide nor hair of her." He sighed and shook his head.

"Now that's too bad," Davy said.

"Oh, that ain't the worst," the stranger went on. "I've got two tads down sick. They need milk the worst way. And I got to find my cow so my young 'uns can get well."

"Why, stranger," Davy cried. "Your cow is as good as found. Me and my dogs will run her down in no time."

Davy and Rattler and Whirlwind hurried into the log. They went up one big limb and down another. They hunted and hunted. It was so dark in the hollow sycamore that lightning bugs came out and hootey owls flew around them.

But there were so many big limbs and they twisted about so, Crockett never so much as got a glimpse, or the dogs a smell, of that cow. At the end of the day he had to come out empty-handed.

There sat the stranger and he looked sadder than ever when he saw Davy. "Oh, my old brown Molly is gone for good," he moaned. "And what will my babies do for milk?"

"Now, don't fret none," Davy said soothingly. "I ain't give up yet a-tall. There's more than one way to call a cow home. Just you wait one minute."

So Crockett went and stood in front of the hollow log. He drew a deep breath and filled his lungs mighty tight. And then he blew.

The air rushing out of his lungs could be heard for miles around. It roared off through the hollow sycamore. And sure enough way down at the little end of the log, the old brown cow came sailing out, mooing most anxiously.

"Oh, thank ye kindly," the man cried, jumping to his feet. "You've saved my young 'uns."

"Why, it wasn't hard," remarked Davy. "I'm always glad to help out folks in trouble. And now I must be gone, for it may be my own two young 'uns are in trouble and need their pappy."

So Davy and the hounds went whistling off down the trail. Davy and Whirlwind whistled *Barbary Ellen*, for it's a fine pretty tune. But Rattler whistled *The British Soldier*, for he liked it better.

And in two days Davy spied his cabin sitting stout and snug in the valley.

Six

Davy looked up into the darkening sky. The comet was half way across the universe looking little and pale. "Fare-ye-well," sang out Davy to the comet. "I'll thank you to trouble us no more."

He swung open the door to his cabin. He and Rattler and Whirlwind stepped out of the cold winter wind into the warm room. A fire blazed on the hearth. Ash cake and bacon were cooking. And Polly and John and William sat on the bench in front of the fire.

And oh, such a welcome as Davy got. Such shouting and hugging and talking you never heard before. Rattler hid under the bed for fear Polly would try to kiss him.

And soon they were eating the good supper Polly cooked. Rattler had two helpings of everything. And when the bowls were empty, Davy turned to his boys.

"Did the rumsquaddle come? Did you fight it off?" he asked.

"Oh, it came all right," cried John. "First we seen its tracks down by the spring. As big around as a barrelhead they were and with long claw marks showing."

"Oh, and we heard it in the night," went on William. "We heard it come sniffing round the window and snuffling at the latch."

"Well, thunderation, you never let it in, did you?" cried Davy.

"Not us!" answered the boys. "But oh, it tried mighty hard to get in. We heard it up on the roof. We heard its long claws a-scratching on the shingles. We heard it moaning and whining round the chimney."

"Well, what did you do?" yelled Davy. "Did you set out the popcorn?"

"Pappy," said John, leaning toward Davy, "YOU NEVER LEFT US NO POPCORN!"

Davy was flabbergasted, for a fact. "Never left you no popcorn!" he exclaimed. "Then how did you get rid of the rumsquaddle?"

"Oh, we did it," chuckled William. "We knew how."

"We heard it on the roof," John told him. "It knocked two stones off the chimney and they fell ker-thump into the fire. So me and William mended the fire. We built it up real good, for we'd fetched in wood a-plenty for Mammy. And when the fire was a-blazing we called up the chimney, 'Come down, old rumsquaddle. Come down and get your popcorn.' And by and by, sure enough, the old rumsquaddle came swooshing down the chimney and fell in the fire!"

"Did he burn up?" asked Davy. "Did he burn to cinders?"

"Why, Pappy, ain't you seen him?" asked William.

"I reckon you didn't know what it was," remarked John. "The rumsquaddle fell down the chimney and set hisself afire. And then he jumped right back up the chimney and kept on going. You can see him plain in the sky. He's all fiery and blazing and he's going so fast sparks keep flying out behind."

Then Davy laughed. He laughed and shouted and stamped his feet. "For," he told Polly, "I've got the finest boys in all creation. They've beat me at every one of my own tricks and got rid of a rumsquaddle without nary a grain of popcorn."

Then Davy pulled two long strings of bear claws out of his shirt front and gave them to his sons. "Here," he said. "Tie these around your necks, for you are mighty warriors and fit to wear these necklaces."

"Ho, Davy, what a heap of bear claws!" cried Polly. "You must have killed a right smart of bears to get so many claws. But where's the skins? And where's the meat? And where's the old grey horse?"

"Well," replied Davy, "it's a long story. I crossed the wide Tennessee into Chickasaw country, and there I come upon bears of all sizes. I killed close on a thousand, I reckon, give or take a few hundred. I skinned the bears and tanned the hides and jerked the meat. And I was loaded up and ready to come home when a terrible thing happened."

The little boys looked at Davy with eyes as big as young gourds.

"I was sleeping sound one night when suddenly I heard a most bodacious uproar in the woods. I jumped up and grabbed my rifle. I looked around and I saw something coming through the woods. And pretty soon a bear ran out. And then here came a deer. And here came a catamount and three bears and a whole heap of deer. And 'coons and 'possums and other little varmints were a-running in and

out of the legs of the big varmints. Snakes were sliding over the ground. And birds were a-flying through the air."

Davy poked the fire and out of the corner of his eye he watched his little boys.

"At first I figured it was a forest fire, for nothing will send the critters running like a fire. But then I knew it was something after them. For far off I could hear it rummaging and a-rooting around in a terrible fashion!"

"What was it?" cried John.

"Was it another rumsquaddle?" asked William.

"Oh, it was worse than a rumsquaddle," answered Davy, and his voice went down, down, down to a deep whisper. "It was an earthquake!"

William got up close to his mammy. And John looked over his shoulder.

"It came closer and closer," Davy went on. "At every step the ground shook and trees wobbled back and forth. The old earth shook till it made a noise like loud thunder. My old horse took fitified and scampered off to Chiny. But me and the dogs stayed to fight the varmint. I got a little grit in my gizzard and I aimed to save my furs and meat."

He paused and the fire hissed at one end of a log. A little puff of smoke shot out.

Then Davy continued, "I loaded Old Betsy with a double charge for I knew I wasn't up against any ordinary critter. And that varmint kept a-clomping nearer. The noise was terrible.

"At the next step the earth split wide open right before our very eyes, and the crack spread along the ground like a black racer snake, straight for us. It was as wide as a young river and went down most nigh to the center of the earth. I jumped out of the way. Rattler and Whirlwind made it too. But I lost all my bear bacons and hams and every frazzling skin I took down in that crack.

"Then big cracks popped open all around us. It was the monstrous weight of the earthquake that split the ground that way. And you should have seen me and the hounds jumping about. Why, we did a reel that would make the fastest fiddler in the nation sit up and take notice. For a spell there, I was so scared we were going to fall in a crack, I plumb forgot about the earthquake."

Davy looked around at them. "But *he* hadn't forgotten us, for there he stood a-flinging rocks and trees and a few acres of good bottom land our way."

"Did you shoot him?" asked William.

Their father shook his head. "I couldn't," he replied. "I couldn't see the pesky thing. There ain't a man living sharp-eyed enough to see an earthquake, I don't reckon. If I could have seen him, I'd have blown his head clean off with Old Betsy. I might have helped him out of his hide with my skinning knife. I might even have heaved a boulder spang at his jaw and laid him low that way.

"I just couldn't see him, try as I might. But boys, he was there all right. I could hear him and feel the earth tremble when he moved. Oh, me and the hounds knew for a fact he was smack beside us. And I began to wonder how in creation we could whip him good enough to make him leave us alone.

" 'Well, if I can't see him, it's the same as if he wasn't there,' say I. 'I'll just treat him that way,' says I. So I gave a big jump and sailed clean through him, *just like he wasn't there.* Oh, he howled like a baby then. He turned around and tore up things fit to bust."

Davy laughed and stretched his long legs toward the fire.

"You see," he said, "I made a big hole in him where I jumped through him. I could see daylight through the hole and it made it a heap easier to tell where he was. But let me tell you I wasn't just standing there flat-footed admiring him. No sirree, for he was after me like a skinned skunk.

"So, I jumped again and made another big hole and that made him even easier to keep up with. I whistled to the dogs and they seen the fun I was having. And they began to jump too. Back and forth we went, sailing high and sailing low.

"That old earthquake bellowed like a stuck buffalo. He turned and twisted, a-grabbing after us. But we never let up making them holes for a single minute. We jumped and leaped till we were well nigh tuckered out.

"And the earthquake was getting weak too, he was so full of holes. One of his hind legs was just about gone, and half of his head and most nigh all his middle. He was getting too weak to holler and stomp anymore. All he could do was snarl and groan a little.

"We kept right on jumping back and forth, hitting the in-between places, till there wasn't anything left of him. Just a few splinters and rags and a wodget of hair, and we shoved them down in one of those big cracks."

"Whew!" cried John and William. "Whew! That was close!"

"It was *mighty* close," remarked Davy. "And things were in a sad mess around there. Trees all down, ground all split open, even the creeks was running backwards."

"Did they really run backwards, Pappy?" asked the little boys.

"They did for a fact," Davy answered. "And that's the reason I didn't get home for Christmas, like I promised. For you see, I had to stay around and tidy up a bit. It ain't a good idea to have creeks running the wrong way. It confuses the fishes. So I went around and tied knots in the creeks so they couldn't flow backwards."

"What about the cracks?" asked John. "Did you fix them up?"

"I had to leave a few big ones," Davy admitted. "But most of 'em I sewed up. I used grapevine thread and a bear's shinbone for a needle. And when I had the rocks piled up and the trees stacked neat as firewood, it didn't look so bad. So I came on home and here I am."

"And we're mighty glad to see you," cried Polly. "Now

you boys get on to bed while I wash up the bowls. Your pappy's got from now till spring to tell you about critters and varmints."

After the boys were asleep, Davy and his pretty wife Polly sat by the fire.

"Oh, Davy," said Polly. "You been in an earthquake and lost all the furs and meat you worked so hard to get. You lost your horse and your cooking pots. Why, Davy, you must have lost your good luck."

Davy smiled. "I can get another horse," he said. "I can go hunting another winter. There for a while I figured I'd lost my good luck too. But I hadn't."

He took Polly's hand. "A man who comes home to a stout safe cabin and all the ones he loves," he told her, "he's the luckiest man in all creation!"